LATIMER STUDIES

16

Gerald L. Bray, Stephen A. Wilcockson
and Robin A. Leaver

LANGUAGE & LITURGY

D1455705

Oxford
Latimer House
1984

BV
178
.B72
1984

CONTENTS

Page

Copyright Gerald L. Bray, Stephen A. Wilcockson and
Robin A. Leaver.

Published by
Latimer House,
131 Banbury Road,
Oxford

ISBN 0 946307 15 6

1 LANGUAGE AND LITURGY

FEW subjects have sparked off more controversy than the vexed question of language in the Liturgy. Recent attempts at liturgical revision may sometimes have been historically reactionary and theologically inadequate, but faults of this kind have scarcely been noticed by those who have made the loudest complaints. For them, it is the quality of expression (or lack of it) which constitutes the greatest obstacle to accepting new forms of worship. Moreover, this view is expressed by churchmen of all schools of thought, who have been nurtured on the classical texts and drawn the substance of their faith from them.

The Linguistic Background

The discussion of language in worship has taken place against a background of linguistic study and analysis which has loomed large in twentieth-century thought, even though many liturgiologists are probably only dimly aware of it. At the heart of the debate is the question of whether a language system governs those who use it, or is governed by them. The argument has strong political and social overtones, in that conservatives prefer the former interpretation, whilst radicals generally opt for the latter.

To appreciate the difference of viewpoints it is instructive to ask whether children should be taught grammar at school. Those who say yes hold the former view, because they believe that a language is a more-or-less fixed system which must be learned. Of course, to some extent usage must inevitably determine what the system is, so that a third-person singular verb will take an -s ending in the present indicative tense (e. g. he gives, not he give) even though it is without any significance logically and is not even paralleled in the past tense (he gave, not he gaves) or in the subjunctive.

Here the pattern of usage is fixed and unalterable, even though it has no logical support. At the same time, supporters of this approach do in fact fly in the face of usage, though almost always in a conservative, archaizing direction. Thus, for example, standard colloquial usage demands contraction in don't, can't etc., but this is not reflected in the written norm, where the full forms are still generally expected. Yet in spoken English, I do not is definitely wrong, since only a foreigner who has learned the language from a book would ever actually say such a thing.

Linked to this is a gray area in which conformity to the written standard is a sign of educated speech. Thus, I am not here would seldom if ever be standard colloquial usage. But I'm not here is regarded as acceptable whilst I ain't here is barbarous, even though it is frequently heard. There is no reason for this, and in many ways it is a pity, since ain't is a general negative which is used for all the persons, e. g. he ain't here. On the other hand, it may be this very simplicity which is rejected as being too crude, and out of line with the positive paradigm, since am never replaces is or are.

People who look for grammatical norms are always having to face choices of this kind, and they can never achieve the logical consistency which they aim for. Because of this, their approach is frequently ridiculed as artificial by educators, who prefer to say that anyone may speak as he likes, as long as he can make himself understood. The shibboleths erected by the prescriptive grammarians are seen as socially harmful, in that they erect class barriers which ought not to exist. The emotional appeal of this approach can be very strong, and it has led to the virtual abandonment of grammar as a subject taught in schools. Its attacks on the classical norms have been well received, especially by those who could never master them, and formerly 'sub-standard' speech and writing is now accepted, and even fashionable!

It is easy to sympathise with this more 'democratic' approach to language, but closer investigation reveals its untenability. Language is communication, which if it is to be effective, must be a shared inheritance. Communication depends on the common acceptance of rules and definitions which make understanding possible. Of course, this can never be perfect, even in a highly unified language like English. There will always be arguments over the exact meaning of particular words in a given context, but unless these are contained within fairly narrow limits, the language will fall apart. Humpty Dumpty believed that he could make a word mean just exactly what he wanted it to mean - and look what happened to him!

Another problem is that of defining a language and its resources. This has loomed as a major question in Bible translation. The Bible is the Word of God, and so many Christians have felt it necessary to translate it into every human language. The trouble is that this is not possible, because many languages do not possess a large enough vocabulary. Sheep, trees and camels are unknown to the Eskimo, so what is the poor translator to do? Either he can invent a word, borrow a word from another language, or find an analogous concept (e.g. seals instead of sheep) and transpose the original text. Each of these methods has been used at different times, and none is fully satisfactory. Even so, linguistic theory now increasingly favours the last of these options, on the ground that it is the one most likely to convey meaning to the hearers.

The process of transposition, known as dynamic equivalence, has also been invoked with respect to English and other established tongues. Here, however, there is a problem which has to be faced which does not exist in primitive languages. This problem is the weight of literary and historical tradition. The English language is capable of expressing a wide range of ideas because it has been developed into a supple instrument of discourse over many centuries. The Bible can be translated quite readily because the concepts which it contains are also present in our language.

4

Or are they? Here there are difficulties with the definition of 'English'. Some Biblical words have no English equivalent, and have simply been transliterated for our benefit. Seraphim, cherubim and Pharisee are obvious examples of these, and hardly anyone knows exactly what they mean, even if most people have a general idea of what they imply. Other words exist in one sense, but have no currency in popular usage - incarnation, atonement, possibly even sin and repentance are examples of these. Words of this kind will be known and used by a minority which is educated and interested in theology. The man in the street, on the other hand, will neither know nor use such terms, even though he will probably realise that they are 'religious'. But he could quite easily use 'religious' words like chapel or covenant without any awareness of their primary association.

What then, is the English language? It can hardly be restricted to the everyday conversation of the 'average' person, since even he (or she) will move into more specialised discourse as and when circumstances require it. Different activities will elicit different responses and usages from the same person, though he may not be conscious of the switch in his own mind. Furthermore, this practice draws on a history of linguistic usage which goes back to the beginnings of the modern English language.

What and when these beginnings were is, of course, more difficult to determine. Convention has established 1500 as a convenient date for the start of the modern period of English, and as a rough guide it is fairly accurate. Old English is definitely a foreign tongue to us, and even Chaucer can be read only with special study.

Shakespeare, on the other hand, is still accessible to us, in spite of a certain exaltedness in the language. We no longer employ the second person singular thou, nor do we use the verb ending -eth (e.g. he giveth). A number of words have dropped out of everyday use or else changed their meaning, so that it is occasionally necessary to be reminded in a footnote of the true sense of certain expressions.

When we compare Shakespeare to the Authorized Version of the Bible, or to the Book of Common Prayer, the astonishing thing is how seldom even an explanatory gloss is needed in the religious texts. Some words have changed meaning, e.g. prevent, quick, ghost, but they are few and far between. The verb forms preserve an archaic flavour but in no way do they impede understanding. The supposition that the classical religious texts are now 'incomprehensible to the majority of worshippers' is a false one. They are perfectly comprehensible to any native speaker of English, and liturgical revisers who imagine otherwise have either been one-sidedly selective in their choice of examples or do not know the history of their own language.

Talk about use of the vernacular in this connection is mistaken, if by vernacular we mean everyday speech. The Reformers never intended to render the Bible or the Liturgy into Tudor cockney, or any other variety of the spoken language. In 1549, there was no English language as we understand it, and what did exist could not have expressed Christian theology with any precision. Different parts of the country used widely different dialects, some of which were mutually incomprehensible. In choosing Home Counties speech as the basis of their translations, the Reformers were accepting the realities of royal power which was concentrated in that area, as well as the tendency of the literary tradition which was then establishing itself. Their work helped to create a linguistic standard which was nobody's native speech. Only slowly has it spread to drive out the dialects and unite the country on the basis of a common norm, which has itself undergone minor modifications. In this sense it is quite true to say that the classical texts do not reflect the spoken tongue, and never have done. On the contrary, they helped to shape the spoken as well as the written standard which is now all but universal.

In terms of vocabulary, the Reformers were unadventurous and seldom successful as translators. English does possess some theological terms, like gospel and atonement, but these are rare beside the vast range of foreign words which were needed to make English capable of theological expression. The fact that we no longer think of nature, grace, person, substance, repentance, conversion and the like as foreign words does not mean that they are not. It means only that domestication has been successful, which in turn means that external borrowing was a real need. To this day, technical theology remains the province of Latin (modified to fit English grammar and speech patterns), and the student has to master a vocabulary drawn from foreign sources. Theology is not unique in this respect of course - the problem is as great, if not greater in medicine, law and the natural sciences!

The real issue at stake, as Ian Robinson has pointed out, is whether Religious English, that particular, immediately recognisable style interlaced with archaisms, should continue as the medium for the public worship of God, or not. And within that style, are the archaisms, which everyone recognises as its most prominent feature, indispensable to it? Can they be removed or modified without destroying the harmony of the whole?

The Assumptions of Modern Revisers
From what has already been said it will be obvious that modern revisers think that only the contemporary vernacular is a suitable vehicle for worship. They justify this position by referring to Article 24, the practice of the Early Church and the language of the New Testament. Let us look at each of these in turn.

Article 24 states that 'it is a thing plainly repugnant to the Word of God and the custom of the Primitive Church, to have publick prayer in the church, or to minister the Sacraments in a tongue not understanded of the people.' It is obvious that the practice being condemned was the use of Latin, not of archaic forms of English, though this point is not always clearly understood. It is also not always noticed that the emphasis is on comprehensibility, not usage. As we have seen, none of the Reformers felt bound to everyday speech as the only acceptable level of English.

The practice of the Early Church, to which Article 24 also refers, is not as straightforward as it might seem. From the beginning, two tendencies are apparent. First, there is the adoption of certain Hebrew and/or Aramaic words as liturgical formulae - abba, maranatha, etc. Not a few of these have survived every vicissitude; even the revisers of 1980 have been content to let all the people say Amen, even though not one in a million could say what it means! Second, there is the universal use of Greek, even by those for whom it was not a first language. Before the third century only heretical groups used other languages, and even then only a few of the more important ones (Latin, Coptic, Syriac and Armenian) became fixed in liturgical usage.

The use of Greek raises the third point made by the revisers, which is that this language was not the classical tongue of Periclean Athens but the common speech (Koine dialektos) of the time. So much nonsense has been written about the koine that it is hard to know where to begin refuting it, but some attempt must be made in view of the importance attached to it as a ground for using colloquial instead of Religious English today.

First, the New Testament may not be written in classical Attic Greek, a fashion which did not become popular until the second century AD, but neither is it a transcription of spoken conversation. To some considerable extent, even the koine was an artificial language, with rules and conventions of its own. Its style owes a great deal to the complex participial phrase structure of classical Attic, a style which could hardly have been the spoken norm. Its vocabulary contained foreign words and solecisms which a native speaker would avoid in writing; we can see the process at work in Luke-Acts, where pure Greek words regularly replace foreign borrowings found in Mark (e. g. hekaton tarches instead of kentourion). Was Luke quenching the Spirit by making modifications like these?

Second, the New Testament contains many different linguistic levels, ranging from the elegant semi-classical Hebrews to the popular, almost demotic Fourth Gospel. The Apocalypse is in a category of its own. There the 'spoken language' is manipulated by the enraptured John to produce a style which is in the world but not of it, and which has frequently baffled insensitive critics, who have seldom been able to advance beyond the charge of linguistic incompetence on the author's part!

Third, the dominant style of the New Testament is not standard koine but the religious Greek which had been developed by the Alexandrian translators of the Old Testament (Septuagint) about 200 BC. This point has been made by L. R. Palmer in his recent book The Greek Language (London, 1980, pp. 195-6). Palmer recognises the popular character of much New Testament language, more so in fact than is justified, but even he speaks of the 'persistent strangeness' which confronts the classical scholar when faced with Jewish and Christian religious writings. There is a special style - Palmer calls it 'translation Greek' - which even Luke adopts as his written medium. The first readers of the Gospels would not have thought that they were 'non-literary' or indistinguishable in style from their everyday speech. On the contrary, they would have been struck by their 'religious' sound, which constantly echoes the distinctive tones of the Septuagint. It is thus quite fair to say that the New Testament writers consciously employed a religious style, interlaced with unfamiliar Hebraisms, as the vehicle of God's revelation to men.

Modern revisers cannot really appeal to history as their justification, but this is only one side of the difficulty they face. The other concerns the definition of the contemporary vernacular. It has already been said that most people move in and out of different linguistic styles according to circumstances, and this is as true of religion as of other spheres of interest. Religious English is not hermetically sealed from the rest of the language, but interacts with it at every level. This is seen quite clearly in the ASB, which has found it impossible to excise words like hallowed or worthily magnify which stick out like sore thumbs to remind us of the linguistic glories we have lost.

Second, modern revisers assume that the standard language of our classical liturgical texts is entirely distinct from the vernacular. They reject the suggestion of overlapping usage or of specialised discourse within a flexible vernacular norm. Instead they offer us linguistic confrontation - 1662 vs 1980. A complex situation is reduced to bipolar opposites, and we are presented with a stark choice which is basically a false one. Of course, the classical language of our liturgy is not everyday speech, but then neither is worship an everyday activity. People in the street do not talk religious language because they are not interested in God. But when the religious dimension does intrude, as at Christmas or at one of the high points of life - birth, marriage or death - the average man expects to hear the religious cadences which he associates with the language of heaven.

I well recall using the BCP at a cremation when I was a deacon. My vicar had instructed me to say 'we commit this body to the purifying fire' instead of 'to the ground', as the text indicates. When the awful moment came, I could not remember the precise words I had been given, so I semi-consciously substituted words I did know, and committed the body 'to the everlasting fire'! Of course nobody noticed the slip, because everlasting is a religious word which sounds appropriate in the context. But had I said 'we're chucking this bag of bones onto the fire', no amount of pleading accuracy or comprehensibility would have saved me from the wrath of the congregation!

Of course, it would be foolish to argue from this that words do not matter or that bizarre theology can be allowed on the ground that nobody really listens anyway! On the other hand, it is equally wrong to suggest that startling, even shocking, forms of speech are the best means of capturing an audience. In the example given above, bad theology slipped by unnoticed, because it had the right ring about it, but matter-of-fact accuracy would have been disastrous. The answer to the mistake cited would not be to change the style so that everybody would pay attention and notice any unfortunate slips, but to make sure that the familiar key, which conveyed the right tone, should also convey the right theology.

The Right Key

Can a composer of modern liturgy use this familiar key to express his thoughts without sacrificing accuracy or comprehension? On what grounds should changes from or modifications in the received texts be admitted for public use? Here the question of taste combines with theology and linguistics, so that it will never be possible to find a style which will please everybody. Nevertheless there are certain principles which whould be borne in mind when literary compositions are to be evaluated and selected or modified for use in church.

The first of these must be the requirement of theological accuracy. Christianity is a religion of the Word made flesh, but without compromising the integrity of either the divine or the human. If liturgical revision can only be purchased at the price of vagueness or inaccuracy in the language, then it should be abandoned. One of the great perils in the search for liturgy in the contemporary vernacular is the lack of precision inherent in popular speech. Most people use words in a fairly loose way, relying on the context or the imagination of the hearers to provide the correct meaning. All literary composition is a struggle against this kind of intellectual sloppiness and the true poet may spend a life time, as Horace observed, honing the rough edges of the native linguistic genius in order to bring out its hidden beauties. There are many levels at which this process takes place, but the definition of terms is among the more fundamental.

In this respect we need give only two or three examples. First, there is the use of the word nature. In many modern translations of the New Testament we are told that Christians have, or are to put on, a new nature, when in fact the Greek text speaks of the new man (anthropos or Adam) and never uses the nature (physis). Does this matter? Yes it does, because nature has a very specific theological meaning (e. g. Christ is one person in two natures), which is not the one intended here. The result is bound to be confusion and misunderstanding, particularly when attempts are made to use this kind of evidence to support the belief that a Christian is automatically entitled to physical, as well as spiritual well-being.

The same word nature is misused in another way in the revised Prayer of Humble Access, where we are invited to pray to a God 'whose nature is always to have mercy'. Here nature has replaced property, presumably on the ground that God is not an estate agent! But this misunderstanding, which incidentally would not be shared by a chemist when speaking of the properties of water, is not removed by the choice of nature as a substitute. God's nature is spirit, not 'to have mercy'. Nor is mercy to be regarded as an attribute of His nature, like omnipotence or infinitude. God does not have to be merciful in order to be true to His nature; He can equally well

9

withhold mercy if circumstances so require. Mercy is always within His
gift, but it is never to be regarded as inevitable, a characteristic of His
nature.

Another example comes from the translation of the Apostles' and the
Nicene Creed, which says conceived by the power of the Holy Spirit. The
words the power of are an interpolation with no justification either
historically or theologically. As the text now stands, it could equally well
refer to the birth of Isaac, which occurred by divine intervention of a
somewhat different kind, or of John the Baptist. Yet this is not what the
Church teaches from the Scriptures! What started as an attempt to explain
the meaning has ended as an open door to false doctrine.

The second principle is that any revision must embody the spirit of the
original. The complete rearrangement of the service in Rite A makes it
impossible to affirm this as far as the liturgy of Holy Communion is
concerned, quite apart from the style of language used. How are we to
maintain that the BCP is the norm of the Church's worship if the services
actually in use bear no relation to it?

At the specifically linguistic level, translation is always a hazardous
exercise,especially when texts of literary merit are involved. A hymn like
Of the Father's love begotten can never be more than a good paraphrase
of the original Corde natus ex parentis ; the most we can realistically hope
for is that the spirit of Prudentius' composition will be substantially
retained, even if the words are not. Another possibility is that an original
text, to which we have no immediate access, will provide the inspiration
for another work of literary merit, though one with a spirit different from
that of the original. Edward Fitzgerald's renderings of The Rubayyat of
Omar Khayyam are the best-known examples of this.

If we look at modern services in this light, their deficiencies are
immediately apparent. What kind of response is and also with you? Why
has this pseudo-colloquial form replaced and with thy spirit? Is it that we
no longer believe that man has a spirit, and that the level of our discourse
is primarily spiritual? We do not go to church just to chat or to wish each
other well.

Likewise you are God, we praise you is a ridiculously inept rendering
of te Deum laudamus . The exalted feel of the original, accurately conveyed
in we praise thee, O God is completely missing from this flat statement
of fact. Do we really have to tell God who He is? This is certainly not
the meaning of the Latin!

Even more serious than this is the revision of popular hymnology
undertaken by the editors of Hymns for Today's Church. They have taken
English texts and rewritten them, to sound 'modern'. As a result,
John Bunyan, the man who went to prison for proclaiming the gospel of
grace now appears in the outlandish dress of Pelagianism!

Some may be terrified
By Satan's testing,
But faith is verified
When we're resisting.
There's no discouragement
Shall cause us to relent
Our firm declared intent
To be his pilgrims.

Spiritual warfare of a rather high order has been made to sound like a Boy Scout outing, with faith being verified like a series of dots on an Ordnance Survey map. It is useless to argue that this effect was not intended - of course not! - but if the original cannot be bettered, why not leave it to survive or die on its own merits and write something new? Better that than a perversion of Bunyan, however unintentional!

The fate of the Pilgrim's Song brings us to the third principle, which is that it is impossible to speak of God in 'ordinary everyday' language and the attempt should not be made. This is, of course, the most controversial point of all, and it requires some defending, apart from the obvious fact that most Christians have always used some form of special language in worship. The reason why this is so is that God is not an ordinary object. Here we reach the heart of our disagreement with the proponents of revision. To them, God should be found in the marketplace - not just be present there, in some hidden way, but found there, in the normal course of life.

A religion which takes God out of the ordinary may have some affinity with the Old Testament, but according to current ideas, is contrary to the witness of the Gospels, in which the Lord appears among men. This sounds fine at first sight, and is frequently used as a justification for streetcorner 'spontaneity' in worship. But wait a minute - Jesus, in His earthly ministry, was found in the highways and byways, but not recognised as Lord and God. When Peter confessed as much, it was the extraordinary nature of his utterance which Jesus commented on, not its everyday quality (Matthew 16:17). Indeed, the only time the Gospels suggest the possibility of worshipping Jesus is in the account of the Transfiguration, an event which by definition was not an everyday occurrence. There is at least as much reason to say that our worship of God should reflect the transfiguration of the ordinary as there is for saying that the contemporary vernacular should be the basis of our liturgical language, and far more, if this vernacular (culled from where - a newspaper?) is supposed simply to be a language suitable for worship.

The biggest practical difficulty in modern liturgical revision is the problem of archaism. Religious language is always archaic to some degree, perhaps because it is the only means we have of transcending time, since we cannot predict how our language will develop in the future. Archaism provides a continuity with the past which is almost timeless in its effect, and it certainly has not been removed from the ASB just by dropping thee

11

and <u>thou</u>. The whole structure of the prayers takes us back at least to the sixteenth century if not beyond, and the modifications made to the language in the interests of modernity do little more than jar on the sensitive ear. The difficulty with archaism is deciding when it becomes incomprehensible. At the time of the Reformation, Latin was felt to be a foreign language in the Germanic countries of Northern Europe, but nobody suggested it was archaic, since it was still in regular use at the academic and diplomatic levels. Latin Europe did not abandon it, at least partly because the foreignness was not felt to the same degree. In Eastern Europe, New Testament (or rather Byzantine) Greek and Church Slavonic have continued to dominate in the liturgy, even though neither language is more than about 60% comprehensible to the average person. But this fact does not destroy the feeling of linguistic continuity, in that neither Greeks nor Slavs regard their liturgical languages as foreign.

They are merely archaic forms of the spoken tongue, and as such have resisted change. It is interesting in this connection to note that Greek Evangelicals, who worship in the modern vernacular, still use a religious language which conforms in every superficial detail to the classical standard. Moreover, in spite of attempts to alter this situation, the resistance has so far proved to be insurmountable. There is something special about the language which becomes flat and even comic when 'updating' is attempted. This is true even when the original is now no longer readily intelligible. An example which will interest readers is the opening line of the refrain to <u>Ho theos as einai meth' hēmōn</u> (God be with you till we meet again). It goes:

Meth'hēmōn kai hymōn
Ho tēs doxēs hēgemōn.

Allowing for sound changes, this is actually sung as:

Meth'imón ké imón
O tis dhóxis iyemón.

Hēmōn (us) and Hymōn (you) are sounded in the same way! Yet to put this into Modern Spoken (Demotic) Greek would make it virtually unsingable, as well as ridiculous in the sound:

Mazí mas ké mazí sas
O Tis dhóxis iyemónas

It becomes 'comprehensible' but loses its rhythm and would provoke laughter rather than reverent worship. Even so, the problem of archaism in Greek is a real one which is having to be faced by both Orthodox and Evangelicals (as well as by Roman Catholics, who now use a semi-modern form of the language as a post-Vatican II replacement for Latin).

In English, on the other hand, there is nothing even remotely comparable to this. Our liturgical language contains archaisms, but in its structure is hardly archaic! We are still in the fortunate position of being able to use it

12

with only a little pruning. Without in any way wishing to encourage the merely clever or pedantic, there is no reason why it should not be polished up and used for the foreseeable future, as the right key for an English-speaker to use in his worship of Almighty God.

Gerald L. Bray

GERALD BRAY is right to call the subject of liturgical revision a 'vexed question', than which 'few subjects have sparked off more controversy.' This has been so for at least two main reasons:

(i) No two people are identical in background, culture and taste, so that it is to be expected that even a shared theology need not lead to shared liturgical preferences.

(ii) Worship is the one activity we cannot opt out of as churchmen. We can inconspicuously steer clear of other practices or policies of our local church with which we feel uncomfortable. However, if the main Sunday worship ceases to suit us, it is easy to feel cheated, alienated and even unchurched.

The deep emotional and psychological roots of both these factors only serve to increase the sense of hurt, loss or outrage. Leading a church into liturgical change is therefore a sensitive undertaking. A church's openness to accept such change is, I believe, a sign of Christian maturity, recognising that other priorities like a concern for mission may have to override personal preferences for traditional worship forms. Willingness to moderate our changes out of love for those whose love of the Book of Common Prayer (BCP) has become part of the very fabric of their devotion also demands maturity and discernment. Moreover, the person who believes in the power of the Gospel and the Holy Spirit as the true drawing power of God will also avoid the false assumption that some have made, that modern liturgy will on its own bring revival or greater numbers to the Church of England.

1. Revision and Replacement

Holding to the reformed theology of BCP, how does one then react to alternative liturgy, especially when it threatens, like the Alternative Services Book 1980 (ASB), not to co-exist with, but effectively to replace the old book? One possible reaction is one of entrenchment, a rejection of substantial revision of our liturgy, desiring either to safeguard its sound theology or to preserve its classical language, or both. Such a view might accommodate a few verbal alterations (e.g. 'go before' for 'prevent'; 'impartially' for 'indifferently') but not so as to make very noticeable alterations to the glories of BCP passages. If I read him correctly, Gerald Bray shows some sympathies with this position. He stresses that 'it is the quality of expression (or lack of it) which constitutes the greatest obstacle to accepting new forms of worship,' (p.3), and holds that BCP classical language is still almost entirely comprehensible. He adds as an axiom of liturgical composition that it is 'impossible to speak of God in ordinary everyday language and the attempt should not be made.' (p.11). This kind of position runs the risk of becoming too inflexible. How long can any one liturgy continue in use before becoming so outmoded in its style and in its assumptions that it loses relevance to a later epoch? How foreign to the average Englishman must it become before substantial revision is deemed necessary? When revision is eventually conceded as necessary, is one then allowed to construct liturgy in contemporary language, and (if not) which period of older English is to be impersonated? And if some alteration is approved, what restraints are to be set on it? Moreover, how far is liturgical entrenchment consistent with the Preface of BCP, which acknowledges in the first paragraph that change in liturgy is proper 'according to the various exigency of times and occasions', since 'the particular Forms of Divine Worship and the Rites and ceremonies' are 'things in their own nature indifferent and alterable'? Finally, to what extent are our cherished feelings for BCP the result of familiarity as much as of anything else - a result which could in principle be achieved by another good English liturgy?

A second, more plausible view of liturgical reform accepts the principle of altering classical forms of worship to a very considerable extent, provided that the theological intent of the original be not lost or compromised. This is a concern for an updating of liturgy so as to hold to the spirit rather than the letter of the old text. In holding this view, many would say that BCP must remain definitive of Anglican theology and worship practices, but may itself now be allowed to fall into disuse in places where evidence shows it to be a less than ideal vehicle of worship for today. Beckwith and Tiller urge that a greater theological consensus within the Church is needed before a revised Eucharist to suit all theological shades of opinion can successfully be achieved, and then add:

> But if such a consensus were reached (it may be asked), would Evangelicals want Prayer Book revision any more than before? The answer is an emphatic yes, and this book may be regarded as an earnest of the fact.[1]

Beckwith and Buchanan add:

> Evangelicals have never been opposed to Prayer Book revision altogether. One or two innocent souls may doubtless be found who see no need for change, but Evangelicals in general are fully aware that a seventeenth century book is not adequate for twentieth century needs.[2]

To look for reform within the theological parameters of BCP, taking due note of the BCP liturgical structures, is to agree with the BCP Preface which asserts that 'common experience sheweth that where a change hath been made of things advisedly established (no evident necessity so requiring) sundry inconveniences have thereupon ensued: and those many times more and greater than the evils that were intended to be remedied by such changes.' This view therefore aims (BCP Preface again) 'to keep the mean between too much stiffness in refusing and of too much easiness in admitting any variation from it.' Gerald Bray's view of the comprehensibility and suitability of 16-17th century English for contemporary worship might lead him to accuse me of 'too much easiness'. However, modernisation within

15

the theological spirit of BCP can (in both theological and linguistic respects, I would judge) fulfil Gerald's own principles of liturgical revision. 'Any revision must embody the spirit of the original, ' we are told, and liturgical revision is described as a lost cause that 'should be abandoned', not absolutely but conditionally; i. e., 'if liturgical revision can only be purchased at the price of vagueness or inaccuracy. ' If, then, discerning revision is allowed, how close to the original must the revision be in order to retain the spirit of it? For instance, does the ASB Communion Rite to 1662 order embody the spirit of BCP by rejecting contemporary trends towards ambiguous eucharistic language typified in Rites A and B, and by retaining some of the BCP unequivocal verbal safeguards against unreformed ideas? Or does it betray the original by changing the order of the first half of the service, and by radically altering the confession, and by shifting and shortening the Gloria? The same may be asked of Beckwith and Tiller's proposed revisions of both the 1662 and the Series 2-3 orders [3] ; they certainly intended to remain true to the spirit of BCP. Gerald Bray sees the complete rearrangement of the service in Rite A as a significant departure from the spirit of 1662, 'quite apart from the style of language used. ' (p. 10). I therefore assume that he would not allow this 'theologically loyal' approach that I am describing too much headway. Those who, with me, argue for liturgical revision within the theological spirit of BCP would not want this point to pass without mentioning in passing that BCP, for all its strengths, does itself contain some defects which can easily be remedied in revision.[4]

ASB is officially an alternative to, not a replacement of BCP, but in practice there are signs that it may become a virtual replacement. What is of concern in this development is not so much the loss of BCP in itself as the fact that ASB is the product of revision which has been pursued from a third position in liturgical intent which makes no real attempt to remain loyal to the spirit of BCP. It is this trend (rather than the modernising tendency itself which Gerald Bray apparently fears) which is the real liturgical threat to biblical, reformed Anglicanism. It is one thing to introduce into Anglicanism unreformed elements of doctrine; it is a step further to frame English liturgy so as to incorporate them into our official documents - and then to impose them, in some instances, on the whole Church of England as the only legal alternative to BCP. Evangelicals may justifiably look to the next review of our liturgy as a time when at least they are released from the unfortunate choice between using the doctrinally sound obscurities of BCP on one hand, or else (on the other) illegally altering offending passages of ASB, rather than blessing inanimate objects or 'entrusting' the departed. Some will want to go further and press for elimination of ambiguity in the Eucharist,[5]   and of blatantly unreformed elements there and elsewhere. If we hold that language ought to express truth rather than veil it, then it makes some sense to ask for there at least to be an alternative we can use without compromise. If we accept the existence of forms which contain prayers for the departed, eucharistic sacrifice language, etc., we are not asking much if we plead for modern alternatives that do try genuinely to remain loyal to BCP doctrine and the plain import of the Articles. The improvement in this respect in the

3. Linguistic Theory and Liturgical Practice

Gerald Bray begins his paper with a consideration of linguistic analysis and the theory of language. He distinguishes those who hold that 'a language system governs those who use it' and 'look for grammatical norms' from those who believe that language is 'governed by them' - i. e. by the users. (p. 3). He attaches great significance to this debate for the controversy over liturgical language. It is, he maintains, 'at the heart of the (liturgical) debate.' The exact tie-up that Gerald sees here between the linguistic question and the liturgical one is somewhat obscured by his immediate introduction of the important but (I hold) distinguishable issue of the use of modern language in liturgy. Gerald's case has some weight if he is here criticizing not the use of modern English in worship but the apparent readiness of ASB to opt occasionally for theologically less than precise terms such as Gerald singles out on p. 9. To my earlier grumbles about points of ASB theology, I would with Gerald add a plea for more caution in making theological statements in a revised liturgy, but in the cases to which we are now referring theological respectability could easily be restored with only slight modifications to the text, and without compromise to the principle of discerning liturgical change. I would say, with respect, that Gerald clouds the issue by introducing as he does the question of modern language into an otherwise interesting point about ASB possibly disregarding important rules of language and meaning.

It is, of course, entirely possible to share Gerald's concern for both sound theology and good English and yet strongly support liturgical revision. Moreover, it is an oversimplification to allege too great a polarity between those who regard themselves as 'governed' by their language and those who think it is 'governed' by them. Gerald Bray himself has to admit (p. 3) that grammatical conservatives cannot achieve complete consistency, owing to language change and variation. Equally, there are not many convinced grammatical anarchists around, either, because some prescribed and mutually accepted grammatical norms are necessary for language to work at all. Classical linguistics was primarily historical in orientation and pedagogic in intent: i. e. it was 'prescriptive' or 'normative', in that it sought to tell us how to speak language 'properly'. This approach to linguistics can be traced as far back as the Greek grammarians. In recent times, linguistics has switched its attention to psycho-social factors, in order to describe how and explain why we do in fact speak the way we do. The replacement of prescriptivism by this descriptive linguistics does not, however, mean the end of grammatical rules. It simply means an abdication of the pedagogy of earlier prescriptive or normative linguists. A modern descriptivist, writing under the heading, 'Linguistics is a descriptive, not prescriptive science', explains,

> It should be stressed that in distinguishing between description and prescription, the linguist is not saying that there is no place for prescriptive studies of language. It is not being denied that there might be valid cultural, social or political reasons for promoting the wider acceptance of some particular language or dialect at the expense of others. In particular, there are obvious administrative and educational

19

advantages in having a unified literary standard...In condemning the literary bias of traditional grammar, the linguist is merely asserting that language is used for many purposes and that its use in relation to these functions should not be judged by criteria which are applicable only or primarily to the literary language. The linguist is not denying that there is a place in our schools and universities for the study of the literary purposes to which language is put. Still less is he claiming to enter the field of literary criticism. This point has often been misunderstood by critics of linguists.[7]

Descriptivism can, in fact, uphold grammatical norms as governing how a language is used in a given context; it does not prefer grammatical chaos. Smith and Wilson, from a descriptivist standpoint, write,

Within modern linguistic theory, to claim that a language is rule-governed is to claim that it can be described in terms of a grammar. A grammar is conceived of as a set of rules which... separate grammatical from ungrammatical sentences, thus making explicit claims about what is "in the language" and what is not.[8]

Since grammatical norms undergo change, so that some aspects of language become first quaint, then alien and finally incomprehensible to later generations, the task of grammar is not only to provide continuity but also to recognize and allow for change. This tension between the historic and the contemporary will always exist in a living tongue, and to some extent there may be disagreement at various stages of development about what is good grammar and what is not. Many inflammable materials now bear the warning 'flammable' due to the common mistake of regarding the prefix 'in' as denoting 'not' rather than 'into'. I still doggedly write 'inflammable' but I may one day have to concede defeat and for the sake of comprehension write 'flammable'. But this does not deny that norms are binding - it would still be wrong to spell it 'flamable' - it merely accepts that to ignore linguistic change is pedantry. When grammar and style have undergone noticeable change, as has English since 1662, the only people who do not feel the archaic quaintness of an old text are those people who are immune to it through frequent recitation and/or a literary frame of mind. Archaisms can then feel familiar, even though these people would not use them in any other context and may not even understand them very well. Admittedly, the language of BCP is far more accessible to today's English speaker than (say) Chaucer. Whether BCP liturgy and AV Scriptures have become quaint, alien or incomprehensible will therefore depend to a great extent on the religious habits and upbringing, or on the literary background, of the worshipper. I would contend that it is fair to describe BCP and AV as quaint and alien to most urban dwellers in Britain today. The grammar of BCP is only part of the problem; style is also very important. Sixteenth and seventeenth century life was hard and work hours were long, but people's approach to life was more leisurely in that people took their time over things. This was reflected in their speech and writing - and in their liturgy whose length and style does not exactly rush to the point. Moreover, the worshipper, who on average would not read most of the liturgy anyway, was much more

impressed by the sound of lofty rhetoric than most of us today.[9] Since
liturgy uses language, it is therefore as important for it to take account of
language change as it is for it to obey grammatical rules. There must be
a common fund of plain meaning within it if it is to do its job in any
generation.

This should not be taken to imply that problems of comprehension are
solved entirely by using contemporary grammar and contemporary good
style in our liturgical texts. Archaism is not the only obstacle to
understanding, although it does exacerbate the problem for most English
speakers who are unused both to tuning in to a strange form of English and
also to the conceptual world of Christian teaching. They have a double
problem. To lift from them the burden of linguistic strangeness at least
frees them to receive patient teaching and explanation of Christian belief.
Modern liturgy such as we have it does retain theological concepts which
are hardly in common coin on Gerald Bray's 'street corner' or 'market
place,' and which are not immediately perspicuous to the new convert or
worshipper. Lack of understanding is therefore more than just a
grammatical phenomenon. There are at least three levels of incomprehension
for the majority of English people when they encounter BCP worship.
    Level One: Cultural alienation - 'I've never heard anything like this in
all my life...I don't fit into this set-up,' etc.
    Level Two: Verbal incomprehension - 'I can't follow these long sentences...
I don't understand some of these old-fashioned words,' etc.
    Level Three: Theological imprecision - 'I thought this was the C. of E.,
not the holy Catholic church,' etc.
It is at levels one and two that liturgy in recognisably modern English can
clear much of the ground that archaic phraseology and vocabulary tend to
clutter up. A modern liturgy helps us to go straight in and tackle level
three incomprehension and confusion in our preaching and teaching from
the Scriptures. Words like 'blood', 'apostolic', 'save', 'advocate', etc.
clearly belong to a technical theological vocabulary and need explaining
and teaching. However, less obviously technical terms also take on a
specialised significance because of their liturgical-theological setting. We
may, for instance, replace 'prevent' with 'go before' (level two adjustment)
but we are then left with the task of explaining what 'go before' means when
applied to an omnipresent God (level three instruction). 'Today if ye will
hear his voice' might be accommodated to the twentieth century by the
substitution of 'you' for 'ye', (level one adjustment) but we have still to
explain what sense 'hear' and 'voice' have in this context (level three
instruction). Since this use of language necessarily recurs frequently in
liturgy, the importance of Bible Lesson-reading and exposition is self-
evident, and the necessity of a modern Bible which itself is linguistically
clear as well as theologically precise is equally obvious. Otherwise we
are back to English appreciation exercises before we can get to the theology
of our texts.

As the Bible is read and expounded regularly, it is this that builds the
world of ideas in which specialised liturgical-theological language becomes
increasingly significant and evocative to the worshipper. Liturgical revision

finds its raison d'etre, not in dragging theological language into common parlance, but in the effort to make theological ideas more accessible to our people, the majority of whom do not possess G. C. E. English, do not read Milton in their spare moments and have not the cultural-religious background to tell them instinctively that BCP, Authorised Version and traditional hymnals are worth persevering with for the treasures they eventually yield. Helped over problems associated with levels one and two, there is no reason why many more English people than at present can readily settle comfortably into the context of worship where level three instruction takes place.

The idea of context is very important in the matter of Christian learning and growth, and is worth pursuing further. Terms used in a specialised theological way are best retained rather than flattened by paraphrase or other simplifying device. 'Save', 'redeem', 'justify', etc. could probably be re-labelled, but only at risk of further problems of theological imprecision or inaccuracy, and of losing the evocative power that they possess. The worshipper therefore needs to take up these ideas, with their various associations, into his growing Christian world-view. This process happens most effectively as a worshipper enters fully into the context of God's people where these terms were born and belong. In worship, we enter not only the context of the local church, but the wider context of all God's people, and 'drink in' the whole dealing of God with his people, both Israel and Church in biblical testimony, and begin to see all fulfilled in Christ and in the outpouring of the Holy Spirit, and witness biblical principles illustrated and worked out repeatedly in the life of the church. It is as he breathes the air of the Kingdom that the language and ideas of the Kingdom start to come alive for the believer. How important it is, then, that the off-putting discomforts and confusions of levels one and two be minimised right at the start of someone's experience of Christian worship. This seems to me a compelling argument for liturgical revision.

Wittgenstein's theory of language and language-learning uses the illustration of learning a game, chess in particular. In order to understand the significance of a chess man, there must be first some concept of the totality of the game. Only then does the role of an individual piece in the game make sense. Words, says Wittgenstein, are like chess pieces in the game of language. The meanings, roles and versatilities of the words are grasped by having a concept of the total language context. In a similar way, it is the total context of the people of God that gives sense to theologically employed terms which occur in liturgy. It is by our being habitually in the context of the worshipping people of God, and, through Scripture, in the whole context of God's dealings with us, that our Christian teaching and learning become most effective. In Wittgenstein's terms, 'one learns the game by watching how others play.'[10] If the new worshipper is going to get into this context, we must help him by providing culturally and linguistically suitable liturgy for him, in a way that BCP now fails to do. Contextual linguistic theory can, of course, appear circular in its reasoning: if the context provides the clue to word meaning, surely this presupposes a prior knowledge of the words if the context is to make sense? This circularity, to some extent inherent in the way that language is picked up, becomes less problematic in the light of 'shared experience', i.e. a fund of ideas, words and perceptions which are already common ground. In the case of liturgy, it means that a certain amount of overlap between what the worshipper is used to in daily speech and what he is being introduced to in the theological world he has entered, allows new learning to begin. A. C. Thiselton comments:

> Understanding begins where there is an area of overlap, or shared experience, between the horizons of the hearer in his present life and the horizons which bound the settings that are determinative for their language and meaning... On the one side, in liturgy, we are using language which draws its operational value from a series of settings belonging to the historical life of Israel and the church. On the other side, also in liturgy, there must be an engagement with the present day life experience of the modern worshipper.[11]

4. With the Mind Also

Language is a vehicle of both expression and communication. These are not always the same thing. As expression, language will often (but need not always) display reasonable perspicuity and significance to the hearer as well as the speaker. Language can, however, be purely expressive in intent, such as we can see in the stock of spontaneous exclamations that are available to us that express pain, shock, anger, fear, surprise, wonder, etc., with the intent of expressing our state of mind rather than of communicating it: we would often say, 'ouch', 'aah', 'ugh', 'ooh', etc., whether or not we had an audience. Something of what we experience in worship lends itself to this category of expressive rather than communicative intent in language. A sense of awe, joy, conviction, penitence, praise, wonder, etc., are deep personal responses to the presence or power of God as he reveals himself through his word or his Spirit. Such responses can defy language, and yet demand expression; the nearest many people get to expressing it is through forms of words or music which are of a higher order than we seek in normal circumstances. Others claim that their charism of tongues comes into its own as a form of supra-verbal linguistic expression. An ideal liturgy will therefore seek to use language that does have the potential to lift us above bald statement and into appreciative expression of religious experience. BCP has for generations succeeded in doing this, by rolling out great phrases, memorable words, moving theological affirmations, which, while making coherent theological statements, are also majestic in expressive quality. At the same time, it ought to be recognised that much of this expressive brilliance stemmed not only from good use of language but also from deep familiarity of worshippers with the Prayer Book from childhood up, and through constant repetition so that the worshipper and his Prayer Book became part of each other. This is so for proportionately few people in this country today. We must also admit that much of the attractiveness of BCP has been that, as an apparently timeless and permanent feature of English religious life, it took on a sentimental status, so that much of its expressive satisfaction masqueraded

as religious experience, but was really more akin to nostalgia. 'These
were the prayers we learnt in childhood... My mother loved this collect... '
It can hardly be claimed for BCP that the expressive satisfaction achieved
by familiarity cannot eventually be equalled by another liturgy, and it can
certainly be said that for the majority of people today BCP is not familiar
at all, and that it will be ever less familiar in the foreseeable future.
Liturgical revisers and all who lead in worship must see to it that liturgy
is composed and read in such a way as to allow language to be a vehicle of
expressing wonder, love and praise.

Without suggesting for a moment that worship is merely a form of (largely
intellectual) self-edification, we must nevertheless remember that language
is a vehicle of communication as well as of expression, and the matter of
effective communication is relevant to the language of public worship.
Primarily, we address God in worship, to whom comprehension of language
form is no problem, but in that he loves to hear his children say things to
him that they understand and mean, we may assume that he is in favour of
worship which is intelligible to as many worshippers as possible. We also
address ourselves in the words of liturgy: 'Bless the Lord, O my soul... '
(Ps. 103:1-5). Worship is, among other things, a self-edifying experience
in which we open ourselves to God by reminding ourselves of his great acts
and by repeating sound doctrines. This in turn serves to feed our sense of
wonder and praise. Hence Paul's stress on edifying the mind (1 Cor. 14:14f).
The question of good comprehension is therefore applicable to the language
we use in worship. We also address one another in worship (c.f. Eph. 5:19;
1 Cor. 14:7-9). The hortatory style of various Psalms, canticles and hymns
involve us in calling to each other; the antiphonal rhythm of versicle and
response, bidding and acclamation causes dialogue between officiant and
congregation. Again, questions arise about what is the most appropriate
language style for our understanding. We also address the wider world in
our liturgy. 'O be joyful in the Lord, all ye lands.' The call to outsiders
to join us in adoring our God is included in our language of worship. A
modern liturgy should not be drafted as a kind of evangelistic tract, but
the simple fact remains that it is at public worship that Christianity in our
land most obviously 'surfaces' for public view. Whether we advocate a
thoughtful approach to BCP or a worshipful contemporary liturgy, we cannot
escape the fact that our worship will be for many their first contact with our
faith. As the established church we need to be particularly aware of this
'outward look' of our worship; indeed, many of our parishioners do drop in
on a casual basis or in an enquiring manner. Paul was very concerned
about the impression given to the outsider by Corinthian worship (1 Cor. 14:
23-25): let us learn from him. Recent church growth findings include the
principle that people 'prefer' to become Christians without having to cross
too many social, cultural or linguistic barriers[12] Eddie Gibbs therefore
pleads for cultural relevance of structures and liturgy in British churches:

Here at home there are denominations which... manifest a cultural
exclusiveness. They impose liturgical traditions... which are alien to
their environment. This is not to say that the world dictates the pattern
for the Church to adopt but to point out that the Church must be constantly

24

examining itself to ensure that it is remaining true to the Gospel and that the only barrier is the inescapable offence of the atoning message of the cross which stands at the centre of that Gospel.[13]

Gerald Bray's point (p. 5) that it is false to say that the old liturgical texts are 'incomprehensible to the majority of worshippers' merely sidesteps the need to consider those of our parishioners who have rarely attended worship, not chiefly out of atheist convictions but because of the image Anglican worship has in their minds. Too many people have experienced it as dull, irrelevant and incomprehensible for us to be complacent. Modern language services can also be dull and lifeless, but they can more easily be made to 'come alive' to the newer worshipper because they put fewer unnecessary obstacles in his way. Gerald's dismissive, 'people in the street do not talk religious language because they are not interested in God,' will surprise many whose pastoral experience indicates that many people's apparent disinterest is directed more at the traditional church than at God, because they feel that the church does not talk language they understand. It may be that Gerald encounters rank disinterest in God in the same places that he finds that our classical liturgical texts are 'perfectly comprehensible to any native speaker of English' (p. 5), but one is entitled to ask if he may have been led to underestimate their spiritual interest because he overestimates their grasp of outdated literary language.

My argument does not entail aiming for the lowest common denominator of language used by those present, nor does it plead for liturgical language devoid of specialised theological terms or lacking in elegant turns of phrase. It does not suggest that newcomers must immediately grasp the full significance of all that is said and done. It merely asks for the kind of overlap between the language and culture of daily life and the special activity of worship for which I argued above. There will therefore be a place for BCP worship in certain traditional 'show-piece' settings, and also in parishes where the culture of the surrounding area demands BCP as the link between people's religious consciousness and biblical Christianity. However, in secularised urban and suburban districts it will be increasingly the case that to opt for BCP liturgy as the main worship form will be to risk dying the death of doctrinally impeccable irrelevance. Our own academic backgrounds and literary tastes can blind us to the chasm that exists between the language of classical liturgy and the conceptual world of the average English speaker today. C. Idle's point about hymns applies to all aspects of liturgical language:

Those with an academic education find it hard to believe the extent to which phrases they take in their stride may be totally misconstrued... Simple (?) lines may not be understood at all. Forms such as 'shalt', 'wilt', 'wert' and 'wast' are especially problematic... It is no answer to talk about dialect survivals, or about singulars and plurals; most people neither use nor understand their native tongue in this way. Anyone disputing this should try to conduct an open discussion of such hymns among ordinary Christians who know their Bibles and indeed their faith but who left school without taking any exams.[14]

How does ASB fare against such criteria? It certainly has theological flaws of a serious nature that one hopes will be ironed out at the next revision, but its theological statements do remain in 'technical language'. Its sentences - generally more manageable in length than BCP - are nevertheless clausal rather than simple, the overall style is more elegant and measured than is usually achieved in conversation, and some of its passages promise to become quite memorable. It is, in short, very far from the 'street corner', 'market place' and 'newspaper' vernacular that Gerald castigates. In ASB, the modern worshipper can find enough of his own recognisable tongue for him to begin to join in the liturgical/theological language-game, and yet at the same time be offered forms of expression and sets of ideas which will lift him above bald statement or trivialising colloquialism. He can be aware of coming out from his everyday world into a higher and greater one, yet not one that is impossibly alien.

It seems to me that this both satisfies Gerald's correct requirement that liturgical language should raise our vision and expectations above 'street corner' level, and also follows broadly the pattern set by N. T. Koine Greek. The exact character of N. T. Greek is not easy to assess because we do not know what Palestinian Koine was like, the papyri being Egyptian. However, it is a fair assumption that the Greek of the N. T. writers owes much to LXX Greek and not merely to the Greek of native Aramaic speakers. The convention of using a reasonably literary Koine to write the N. T. texts, and the inevitable influence of LXX renderings do not, however, tell us that early Christian worship was linguistically poles apart from what ordinary converts could readily join in and understand. Indeed, the history of the Gentile mission in Acts suggests that the church went out of its way to break down cultural and ritual barriers that were not essential to faith and order. N. T. Koine would have sounded serious, weighty and religious to a first century Greek speaker, but it would have been readily understood in terms of its grammar. L. R. Palmer's conclusion is worth quoting:

It was, of course, the language of everyday life and not the artificial literary language that the new religion used to reach the hearts of converts once it had spread beyond the frontiers of its native Palestine. The language of the New Testament was for long regarded by scholars as sui generis , a religious language that had evolved separately from the secular koine, a view natural enough since, as a literary form, the Gospels were unique. However, study of the contemporary inscriptions, and in particular the papyri, showed that the language of the New Testament is, by and large, close to that of the popular language as reflected in the non-official papyri. This finding is not affected by the notable differences of style between the different authors, Luke the Greek physician being the most careful stylist... Yet, despite his greater mastery of Greek, Luke also preferred to write his Gospel in language closer to the speech and to the hearts of the people. This evident fact is highlighted by the contrasting tone and style of the long and elaborate period which forms the Prologue addressed to Theophilus.[15]

The contemporary liturgy offered by ASB does retain a mainly literary and theological style and yet is far closer than BCP to the speech and hearts of ordinary people. It is not, therefore, a betrayal of our inheritance to claim that, given a more faithful allegiance to BCP theology, and more careful attention to some theological terms, we have reason to look for the day when a contemporary Anglican liturgy may replace the BCP in many if not most of our churches. None of Gerald's arguments are sufficient to undermine the attempt to open up for today's England a form of Anglican worship which offers reverent praise, faithful teaching, sound theology, good language and effective communication.

Stephen Wilcockson

FOOTNOTES TO WILCOCKSON

[1] R. T. Beckwith and J. E. Tiller, The Service of Holy Communion and its Revision, Marcham Manor Press, 1972, p. 22.

[2] R. T. Beckwith and C. O. Buchanan, 'This Bread and this Cup: an Evangelical Rejoinder,' Theology, June 1967, pp. 266f., quoted in ibid., p. 22.

[3] op. cit., pp. 104ff.

[4] Beckwith and Tiller, whose approach to BCP is sympathetic, list about ten such defects which arise in BCP due to theological blinkers of 16-17th centuries, or else from socio-political conditions that no longer obtain. See ibid., pp. 90-99.

[5] The introduction to Series Two declared: 'We have also, where matters of eucharistic doctrine are concerned, tried to produce forms of words which are capable of various interpretations... and each will be able to interpret according to his own convictions.' (An Order for Holy Communion, London, S. P. C. K., 1966, p. viii).

[6] C. Idle, Hymns in Today's Language?, Grove Books, 1982, p. 13.

[7] John Lyons, Introduction to Theoretical Linguistics, Cambridge, 1968, p. 42, section 1:4:3.

[8] Neil Smith and Deirdre Wilson, Modern Linguistics, Pelican, 1979, p. 14.

[9] A point made by Dr. Stella Brook in her (cautious) approach to liturgical revision in Liturgical Reform: Some Basic Principles, C. I. O., 1966, pp. 14ff.

[10] L. Wittgenstein, Philosophical Investigations, sections 19, 23, 88, etc.

[11] A. C. Thiselton, Language, Liturgy and Meaning, Grove Books, 1975, p. 8.

[12] See (e. g.) D. McGavran, Understanding Church Growth, Eerdmans, 1970, pp. 198ff.

[13] E. Gibbs, I Believe in Church Growth, Hodder and Stoughton, 1981, p. 123.

[14] op. cit., p. 11.

[15] L. R. Palmer, The Greek Language, Faber and Faber, London, 1980, pp. 194ff., c. f. Matthew Black, 'The Biblical Languages' in The Cambridge History of the Bible, Vol. 1, ed. P. R. Ackroyd and C. F. Evans, Cambridge University Press, 1970.

THE two foregoing essays originated within the Latimer House Theological
Work Group. They represent two approaches to the common problem of
liturgical language and reflect the wider debate within the Church of England.
One stresses the riches of the Book of Common Prayer and the inadequacies
of the Alternative Service Book, whereas the other outlines the strengths of
the ASB and the weaknesses of the BCP. The apparent polarization
approximates to the either/or situation that is common throughout the country.
Worship is either according to the BCP or the ASB. But the issue of
liturgical language is far broader than the choice between a liturgical book
issued in 1662 and another in 1980. Nor is it simply a matter of linguistics.
The title of Gerald Bray's essay reflects current thinking: Language and
Liturgy, with the stress on language. The contemporary debate has become
preoccupied with language and communication problems. We have become
obsessed with the technicalities of language at the expense of its meaning
and content. The emphasis should rather be the other way round, hence
the title of this postscript.

The language of worship is a part of liturgiology, which is itself a branch
of theology. Therefore liturgy and the language of liturgy need to be discussed
within the framework of theology, which both the authors here clearly
understand. But all too often the language of liturgy is considered in isolation,
with the result that liturgies, hymns, prayers and inclusive-language
lectionaries have been drawn up which contain theological inconsistencies
and nonsenses. For example, the inclusive (= non-sexist) language issue -
on which, strangely, both authors make no comment - has caused and is
causing enormous problems on the other side of the Atlantic. Certainly
there are instances when a masculine gender can and should be avoided,
but when the Fatherhood of the First Person of the Trinity and the Sonship
of the Second Person are called into question on linguistic grounds it has
ceased to be a semantic problem. At root the debate is essentially
theological, and instead of playing liturgical word-games and working out
the implications afterwards, we should rather be establishing first what
it is we want to express in our worship - and why - and then seek to express
it in an adequate language which will convey what we mean.

All too often the theological dimensions are passed over and the subject
of the language of liturgy is discussed simply as communication. Thus it
is concluded, on the one hand, that the BCP is 'bad communication' because
it uses a vocabulary which is thought to be heavily redundant and the ASB
is 'good communication' because its language is accessible and up-to-date.
Or, the BCP is thought to be 'good communication' because its vocabulary
has religious overtones whereas the ASB is 'bad communication' since its
language is modern, flat and prosaic. There may well be elements of truth
in all these opinions but the analyses are far too superficial. It is true that
the language of the ASB is frequently imprecise and ambiguous, but the BCP

is not entirely free from ambiguity either. An example would be the Prayer
of Humble Access: taking it at face value, just exactly what is the eucharistic
theology which lies behind it? Similarly it is often stated that the language
of the BCP is full of Biblical imagery and content. But the same could be
argued for the ASB, indeed, the Dean of Worcester has stated that in the
light of the 'intense Biblicism of the modern rites' the need is for 'carefully
chosen hymns...to fill up the devotional desert which will otherwise exist
between the world of the Bible and that of our own day' (T. Baker, 'New
Hymns for New Liturgies', Hymn Society Bulletin, Vol.9, Jan. 1981, p.185).
The BCP advocates would say that the 'devotional desert' is made fertile
and lush only by the language of the Prayer Book. But if worship has a
totally antiquarian sound the implication that is carried over to the modern
worshipper is that somehow the Christian faith, and its expression, was
more effective and relevant three hundred years ago than it is today. This
is exactly the argument of many advocates of the ASB. It is because the
BCP speaks in a language different from our own that we need a modern-
language liturgy to speak to our needs today. But the danger here is that
we can easily give the impression by our modernity that we are the first
Christians who have discovered the secrets of Christian worship, and we
did so no earlier than this morning. Perhaps the antithesis is overstated,
but the point is valid and needs to be made: our worship should reflect both
the continuity from the past and the contemporaneity of the present, and it
is desirable that these elements should be evident in the language we use.
For example, Martin Luther, in seeking to meet the liturgical needs of
the church people of Wittenberg, insisted that the new hymns he and his
colleagues were writing should 'avoid the language used at court' and, 'in
order to be understood by the people, only the simplest and most common
words should be used' (Letter to Georg Spalatin, dated towards the end of
1523; Luther's Works, Vol.49, p.69), yet when he came to put the liturgy
into the vernacular in the Deutsche Messe of 1526 he included the Kyrie
eleison untranslated (ibid., Vol.53, p.72). Thus worship in Wittenberg
was a marvellously rich experience which included the continuity from the
past in the Greek Kyrie eleison, ecclesiastical Latin and German folk-
hymns (though with additional stanzas) from the previous centuries, and
the contemporaneity of the present in the newly-translated German Bible
and liturgy, and the new hymns written by the Wittenberg circle of hymn
writers. Although some would argue that this was a transitional phase as
the Reformers worked their way into new liturgical forms, Luther himself
never thought that way: he self-consciously attempted to blend the old and
the new.

No doubt the editors of Hymns for Today's Church would argue that this
was just their intention; that their revisions are an attempt to blend the old
and the new. While some of their revisions of older hymns are quite
successful, many are disturbing to the ear because they have tried to make
them speak as if they were contemporary expressions of praise and prayer.
This is where I would take issue with Stephen Wilcockson who has not really
taken Gerald Bray's point that revision should embody the spirit of the
original. Simply to state, as do Stephen Wilcockson and Christopher Idle,
that it is nothing new to revise hymn texts because practically every hymn

book editor in the past has done so, is too superficial. Certainly hymn
book editors - John Wesley being the worst, or best, depending on how you
look at it! - have modified hymn texts, but have done so for theological
and/or poetic reasons. In other words, these revisions were within the
spirit and style of the original texts.[1] What is a new departure in Hymns
for Today's Church is modernisation of the language of practically all its
hymns - alterations which are often inconsistent with the spirit and style
of the originals. Now the older hymns speak with the same accents and
vocabulary as the new hymns. The strength of the older hymns, which
made their impact on us simply because they did not use the same language
as we do, has been seriously weakened. We need the witness from the past
which is expressed in a language that makes us stop and think more deeply
than some modern facile expressions do. Of course, if the language has
become too antique, inaccessible and incomprehensible then it should be
consigned to historical anthologies and replaced by something else, newly
written - which is just the argument many advocates of contemporary-
language liturgies would use. They would say that liturgical language
which has come to us from the past has become unusable (whether it has
all become 'unusable' is rarely debated). It is 'culturally conditioned'
language which reflects thought-forms and presuppositions which are quite
different from ours today, in the latter part of the twentieth century.
Since our cultural environment is different from that of the past, it is
argued that the language must be changed in order to make liturgical worship
appropriate and approachable in our day. In other words, the language of
the liturgy must be demythologized from its antiquated cultural and linguistic
conditioning and remythologized in contemporary terms. But to speak of
'demythologizing' takes us out of the sphere of linguistics into the area of
theology, and the mention of 'cultural conditioning' takes us into the arena
of the arts, for culture is expressed through the arts. We have thus moved
into the ambit of theological aesthetics.

The question of liturgical language is not simply confined to what is to be
communicated but also includes how the message is to be communicated.
That is the meaning of the beginning of the Prologue to St. John's Gospel.
God had something to say, the Word, and he expressed that Word in and
through his Incarnate Son. In worship we have something to say, but it is
important for us to consider how we are to express what we mean. However,
our preoccupation has been mainly at the communication level. An example
is the popularity of family services - which in a sense can be seen as a
reaction against the language of the BCP - over the past twenty or thirty
years. A feature of these services has been the extensive use of visual-
aids for the talk - though many of the examples I have seen should be called
verbal-aids, since they make excessive use of the alphabet. But where
visual forms have been used, they have been generally diagrammatic and
factual rather than artistic and 'uplifting', for want of a better word. The
stress has been on communication: it apparently does not matter how ugly
or inartistic the pin-men on the blackboard are so long as the message gets
across. But how we express the message in visual terms affects the way
it is received. Are we not guilty of cheapening the Gospel, and of taking
the sense of the wonder of God's grace out of our worship, by the slovenly

use of a few lines on a blackboard, overhead projector-slide, or whatever?
A parallel can be drawn with regard to the language we use in worship.
For many, communication is the top priority: it does not seem to matter
what words we use so long as the message gets across. But again, the
words we use affect the way in which the message is received.

I would want to stress again that communication is but one part of the
problem and that we are in the province of theological aesthetics, which
ought to make us also think theologically of how what we want to say is to
be communicated. For example, the Biblical doctrine of creation reminds
us that God was pleased with the universe he created and saw that it was
good in all its detail. We know from our own experience of it that God's
creation is exceedingly beautiful: the colour, form and expanse of the
natural world often takes our breath away. Therefore, as we come to
worship God as the Creator of all that is good and beautiful - since we,
too, are part of his creation - we will not be satisfied with the first words
which come into our heads. The language of our worship will reflect our
God-given creativity as we express our praise, prayer and devotion in as
significant a way as possible.

The doctrine of salvation has a similar thrust. St. Paul writes (1 Corinth.
5:17) that 'if anyone is in Christ, he is a new creation; the old has gone,
the new has come!' Therefore, when we come to worship our God who has
redeemed us in Christ, our language, as well as our very selves, will
reflect the new creation of his grace. We shall thus not be content with
simply repeating our ordinary, everyday language in our worship. We
need to articulate our response of faith and commitment to our God who has
forgiven us in Christ, and therefore we feel the necessity for an expanded
vocabulary which has 'salvation' overtones: 'grace', 'atonement',
'reconciliation', 'justification', and so on. Indeed, if we ourselves are
to 'become the righteousness of God' (2 Corinth. 5:21), that righteousness
ought to be reflected in the language of our worship. Further, it is
significant that St. Paul, when speaking of the worshipping activities of
rejoicing in prayer and thanksgiving in Philippians 4:6, goes on to exhort:

Finally, brothers, whatever is true, whatever is noble, whatever is
right, whatever is pure, whatever is lovely, whatever is admirable -
if anything is excellent or praiseworthy - think about such things.
(Philipp. 4:8)

It therefore follows that the language of our worship should at least attempt
to approximate to whatever is true, noble, right, pure, lovely, admirable,
excellent and praiseworthy. Of course, that does not mean that it has to
be therefore inaccessible to the ordinary man. Liturgical language may
be an art-form but it is both a theological and a popular art-form - it
includes the doctrine of the priesthood of all believers as well as the
doctrine of God. St. Paul was equally clear that he would 'rather speak
five intelligible words... than ten thousand words in a tongue', and insisted
that 'tongues' should be interpreted so that all should understand (1 Corinth.
14:19-28). There is no simple equation that maintains that basic language

is ugly and cultured language beautiful, since we know only too well from experience that the opposite is often true. A simple vocabulary can be used to express thoughts in a beautiful manner - indeed, the most effective poetry is often just that. Again, it is not simply what is expressed but also how it is articulated.

The purpose of worship, and thus the language of worship, is to proclaim God's initiative in universal and personal history and to unite the response to God's initiative of those who gather together for worship. It is therefore both an expression of the doctrine of the priesthood of all believers and of the doctrine of the communion of saints. It recognises that the personal salvation-history of the worshippers is earthed in the universal salvation-history of all God's people. It is thus a continuation of Hebrews 11 into the present. If the language of worship comprises only the language of previous generations, liturgical worship will degenerate into a rigid incantation of unaltering formulae - a similar effect would be achieved if we only used Gregorian chant, or only the music of Palestrina, for the liturgy. If, on the other hand, the language of worship is purely contemporary in form and idiom, acts of worship will become merely existential experiences which have roots neither in theology nor history - as if we were to use only contemporary music - pop or atonal - for our worship.

Liturgical language should be as rich and varied as liturgical music. Gregorian chant - and Anglican chant, for that matter - can co-exist alongside the contemporary responsorial psalm; the music of Palestrina and/or Victorian hymn tunes can be included in the same service as the church music or hymn tunes of, say, Herbert Howells, Peter Cutts and Norman Warren. The language of our worship should therefore express both the continuity and the contemporaneity of the faith and should be rescued from the sterile polarity of the either/or debate.

Robin A. Leaver

FOOTNOTE TO LEAVER

[1] That is not, of course, to suggest that John Wesley did not indulge in the modernisation of the language of hymn texts. There is evidence to show that over the years the hymn books he and his brother Charles edited gradually exhibited less and less archaic spellings in favour of simpler, 'modern' forms. Further, in the first 'Methodist' hymn book of 1780 'ye' is often rendered as 'you', but there was no systematic policy of modernisation. For example, line 3 of stanza 3 of Hymn 6 in that collection runs 'He, who all your lives <u>hath</u> strove.' In John Wesley's manuscript draft of 1778 the line is given as '...your lives <u>has</u> strove', but the modernisation never appeared in the printed hymn book (see The Works of John Wesley, Vol.7: A Collection of Hymns for the use of the People called Methodists, edited by Franz Hildebrandt and Oliver A. Beckerlegge with the assistance of James Dale, Oxford: Clarendon Press, 1983, p.87 and footnotes.). Even Wesley could have his lapses and, like other hymn book editors who have followed him, could not refrain from changing a small detail which he should have left well alone. Take the same line noted above: '<u>He</u>, who all your lives...'. The original, which first appeared in 1742, ran thus: '<u>God</u>, who all your lives...' By this casual emendation John Wesley destroyed a carefully devised pattern of words his brother Charles had created in the previous two stanzas:

> 1. Sinners, turn...
> God, your Maker...
> God, who did your being give,
> ....
>
> 2. Sinners, turn...
> God, your Saviour...
> God, who did your souls retrieve,
> ....
>
> 3. Sinners, turn...
> God the Spirit...
> <u>He</u>, who all your lives hath strove,
> ....